I0569299

Rising 100 Meditations, Affirmations and Prayers for Military Families

Rising 100 Meditations, Affirmations and Prayers for Military Families

MICHELE P. ELLISON, A.C.S.W., M.DIV.

Kravitz & Sons
INNOVATORS IN PUBLISHING, MARKETING AND ADVERTISING

The information and solutions offered are the result of personal and clinical work applications and are intended to serve as guidelines, and not as a replacement of professional consultation or therapy. Please discuss specific situations with your religious leader, spiritual director or mental health professional. Any use of the information is at the owner's discretion. The author makes no representations or warrantees that any individual will receive a particular result. Any and all expressed or implied warrantees are disclaimed. The author specifically disclaims any and all liability arising directly or indirectly from the use or application of any information contained in this book

Kravitz and Sons LLC
1301 Farmville Blvd, Suite 104
Greenville, NC 27834

© 2025 Michele P. Ellison, A.C.S.W., M. DIV. All rights reserved.

No part of this book may be reproduced, stored in a retrieval system, or transmitted by any means without the written permission of the author.

Published by Kravitz and Sons LLC.

ISBN: 979-8-89639-301-6 (sc)
ISBN: 979-8-89639-300-9 (e)

Library of Congress Control Number: 2025909385

Because of the dynamic nature of the Internet, any web addresses or links contained in this book may have changed since publication and may no longer be valid. The views expressed in this work are solely those of the author and do not necessarily reflect the views of the publisher, and the publisher hereby disclaims any responsibility for them.

This book is dedicated to the Glory and Furtherance
of the Kingdom of God through the Gospel of Jesus the Christ.

In memory of my

Father
James Monroe Ellison, Jr.
Founder and Commander of Veterans of Foreign Wars Post 361 and
Mother
Ruby Miles Ellison
President of the Ladies Auxiliary V.F.W. Post 361

and

In recognition of all those who have served and their entire families.

ACKNOWLEDGEMENTS

———⋯◦✦◦⋯———

First acknowledging God, the Creator, Redeemer and Sustainer of my life. All praises and thanks to the LORD God. I thank God for the life journeys and stories of military and intelligence friends and families that I have shared; and for those I have provided spiritual care for throughout the years.

A special thank you, to all military personnel and their families, who have been there for me from my birth to the present day.

Thank you to my typist Pat Kaley of Kaley Secretarial Services, Reginald Roberts, and my publicist and publisher.

Thank you for purchasing this book. The blessings of God be with you. Ten percent (10%) of royalty proceeds donated to military related charities.

INTRODUCTION

———⊸∘⟨⟨⟩⟩∘⊶———

This devotional meditation book has been in the making for some time. Through much prayer and meditation it is delivered to you now. With some skill I have integrated mental health healing techniques and spirituality into a book of meditations with affirmations and prayers.

Military families have a variety of experiences, depending on whether their love one is active, in- active, reserve, discharged or retired. The families, both nuclear and extended are all impacted for a lifetime. These meditations are for us.

How to Use This Book

There are 100 total meditations, affirmations and prayers. The best way to use this book is to read one meditation per week. Read the entire Scripture for the day. Read the entire meditation and say the **affirmation** 3x daily for one week. Let the Scripture, **affirmation** and prayer soak down into your being during the week. If you have any thoughts, make note of them on the provided page. After one week, move on to the next meditation,

I present to you *Rising -100 Meditations, Affirmations and Prayers.*

May the grace and peace given through Jesus the Christ, which are beyond all human understanding, keep our hearts and minds.

Blessings.

TABLE OF CONTENTS

MEDITATION 1

Esther 4:1-17

There "For Such a Time as This"

And who knows whether you have not come to the kingdom for such a time as this. v.14b

We are military families, and descendants of previous military personnel – we are family, there for our loved ones and our nation "for such a time as this."

We are on the move all times of day and night. While others sleep, our loved ones are on the move in missions here and around the globe.

We are in prayer.

Because we know, what we know, we are on the move, in our households, faith groups, in every profession and occupation in this nation for the healing and protection of our lives, our nation and humanity.

We are all here in place "for such a time as this." - Strategically Placed by God.

Affirmation: I am an instrument of the living God to be used for His Glory.

(Repeat the **affirmation** 3 times out loud)

Prayer: O Lord, we thank you for being with us during this spiritual battle in the universe. Grant us healing in Christ and the peace of Christ that passes all understanding. Empower us through the working of your Holy Spirit to be your disciples and instruments in the world today.

Reflections / Notes

_____

_____

_____

_____

_____

_____

_____

_____

_____

_____

_____

_____

_____

_____

_____

_____

_____

_____

MEDITATION 2

Matthew 5:13-20

Salt

You are the salt of the earth, but if salt has lost its taste, how can its saltiness be restored? ...It is no longer good for anything, but it is thrown out and trampled underfoot. v.13

Salt is a preservative of food, giving it a longer lifetime to be eaten. Salt is a mineral that is used in healing, to relax muscles and heal injuries. Salt is used to clean impurities from plants, animals, and human beings. The proper amount of salt creates a chemical reaction that balances the human body's chemistry.

Jesus calls His disciples the "salt of the earth."

We preserve life on earth. We bring balance to systems – government, religious, family, community, societal institutions and traditions. We are in the earth to bring healing (body, mind, soul and spirit) including justice for the oppressed as defined by Scripture.

God empowers us through the working of the Holy Spirit to be "salt" that fulfills its purpose.

Affirmation: I am salt.

Prayer: O Lord, empower me by the working of your Holy Spirit to be the 'salt' you intended for me to be.

Reflections / Notes

_____

_____

_____

_____

_____

_____

_____

_____

_____

_____

_____

_____

_____

_____

_____

_____

_____

_____

_____

_____

MEDITATION 3

Daniel 4:19-37

Going Higher

...I Nebuchadnezzar, lifted my eyes to heaven, and my reason returned to me. v.34

As military families sometimes we can forget who is ultimately in charge. Who can ultimately turn-the-tide, turn the tables, blowing the ultimate wake-up and victory horns. It is not all in our human hands and wills, although a lot has been given to us to do and perform within our disciplined lives.

Nebuchadnezzar believed all his success came from within himself. He worshipped himself and all he had achieved. He worshipped himself and his mission, not God – Most High whose kingdom endures from generation to generation into eternity and who has determined the ultimate mission with all its strategies, goals, objects and benchmarks.

Affirmation: Within the changes and chances of life, let us lift our eyes to heaven and by so doing; bring sanity to our lives and the lives of those we love.

Prayer: O Lord God, lead me, guide me. I worship you as the only Sovereign Lord of the Universe. Keep me and those I care about surrounded by Your love and care. May we be victorious through You.

Reflections / Notes

_____

_____

_____

_____

_____

_____

_____

_____

_____

_____

_____

_____

_____

_____

_____

_____

_____

_____

MEDITATION 4

Matthew 8:28-9:1

Deliverance from the Demonic

...and He said to them "Go!" So they came out... v.32

I remember reading in the newspaper that there was a debate on whether to put the Satanic symbol on a military tombstone since the veteran had been a confessed Satan worshiper. Traditionally, religious symbols of the Cross of Jesus Christ or Star of David were placed on tombstones.

Imagine working alongside someone who worships Satan, and the spiritual flow of spirits that could take place.

I remember the eyes of a person in my life when he would become violent. They were like a flame. I would say I bind you in the name of Jesus; and peace would come upon the situation.

Some spirits come out over time, only by prayer and fasting. Other spirits must be exorcised by those who are trained to do so.

Beyond the human condition and its frailties, if you believe you are being tormented by the spiritual forces of hell, turn to those ministries of Jesus Christ that can help you.

Affirmation: I am delivered from all evil, in the name of Jesus.

Prayer: O LORD, thank you for your deliverance from every foothold and spirit of the powers of evil.

Reflections / Notes

_____
_____
_____
_____
_____
_____
_____
_____
_____
_____
_____
_____
_____
_____

MEDITATION 5

Genesis 1:26

Order Out Of Chaos

...darkness covered the face of the deep, while the spirit of God swept over the face of the water. v.26

In ancient mythologies, 'water' – the deep can symbolize chaos. Rough water can speak about our environment or what we experience deep within our bodies, needs, hearts, emotions, relationships with others and/or with God.

In the beginning, God spoke and there was light. God still speaks to the chaos in our lives, bringing light so we can see more clearly and deeply - calming rough seas.

God helps us recover from the chaos that sweeps over our lives and lifts us to another place of faith, peace, love, and hope.

Affirmation: God is with me.

Prayer: O LORD God may Your Spirit sweep over the waters of my life, and the lives of those I know, and bring light, love, faith and hope. Among the many voices in our lives, help us to hear and follow your voice. Speak deep within and through others.

Reflections / Notes

MEDITATION 6

Mark 12:30

Loving the Lord Your God

You shall love the Lord your God with all your heart, and all your soul, and with all your mind and with all your strength. v.30

In a world where many things can take first place in our lives, we are called to love God above all else. Many will say "Well, God will forgive me if I don't". And God does forgive us; and the expectation is that we will not willfully repeat over and over again the same sin. We rise in the strength and inner sinew that God gives us. We rise in the power of the Holy Spirit and move from one degree of glory to the next.

Filled with the love that comes from loving the Lord our God and God's love for us, we are able to surmount what seems at times to be unbeatable odds, turning our lives, the lives of our loved ones and others around us to obedience to God above all else.

Affirmation: I will love the LORD my God with all my being.

Prayer: O Lord, help me to love You above all else, so there will be undying meaning, comfort and support in my life.

Reflections / Notes

MEDITATION 7

Mark 12:31

Loving Yourself

You shall love your neighbor as yourself. v.31

Loving God, leads to loving yourself and loving your neighbor as you love yourself.

The question becomes at some point in our lives – Do you love yourself? No matter what has happened, can you say I know who I am? Do I know who God says I am? Many people do not feel comfortable with themselves. What they have become. How they live their lives. There is a biting edge on how life is lived.

God meets us where we are and says to each of us, "I the Living God love you. I forgive you for not being completely all I have desired you to be. This is a new day. Welcome back. I will teach you to love Me, love yourself and love your neighbor".

Affirmation: I will love God. I will love myself. I will love my neighbor.

Prayer: O LORD, help us to make you not just our Savior, but our LORD.

Reflections / Notes

MEDITATION 8

Romans 13:8-10

Love One Another

Owe no one anything, except to love one another.... love does no wrong, to a neighbor.

Loving another human being is not always easy. Sometimes there is a conflict in values, in behaviors, within occupations. What do we do? Some try to relieve the conflict through suicide. Some self-medicate with drugs and alcohol. Some do the group thing for comfort, a sense of belonging – even if the group thing is questionable.

At the end of the connecting, we are left facing the God of the Universe, and trying to be instruments of God's peace and love within our families, communities, nation and world.

Affirmation: I am an instrument of God.

Prayer: O LORD, empower us to love and persevere.

Reflections / Notes

_____

_____

_____

_____

_____

_____

_____

_____

_____

_____

_____

_____

_____

_____

_____

_____

_____

_____

Meditation 9

Psalm 18:20-30

Humbling Yourself Before God

*For you deliver a humble people, but the haughty eyes you bring down.
v.27*

Knowing that God is on your side gives you tremendous strength, gratitude, focus, fortitude, and determination.

Kneeling in prayer or praying before you rise, and when you go to sleep at night can be sobering experiences. It can place your human finitude before the God of the Universe and help you to rise up in God-given strength. You learn the promises of God, God's deliverance and refuge. And yes, God does move in your behalf. Prayer during the day can help you maintain mental, emotional and spiritual balance. You come to know that God does far more than you ask or think.

Affirmation: I humble myself before You O Lord, God of the Universe.

Prayer: O LORD, may I always remember that you are the God of the Universe, not me. Empower me to be Your partner.

Reflections / Notes

John 13:31-35

The Mark of the Disciple

By this everyone will know that you are my disciples, if you have love for one another. v.35

Love is more than a feeling, more than romantic connection, more than acts of kindness. It is a commitment to how we treat one another in a touch, a tone of voice, an embrace, a glance, a nod of the head, the nurturing. It is about being a love-filled presence; and a presence even when you are not in the same physical location.

We are not always at our best, but we are called to accept the forgiveness of God for not being loving as we ought, and to get better at our loving. Sometimes the most loving thing to do is to have "tough love" in the now, for a better love of self and others in the future.

Even Jesus said good-bye to His disciples, so they could experience a different type of love in the future.

Affirmation: My love for others is increasing.

Prayer: O LORD, empower and teach us to love as we ought.

Reflections / Notes

_____

_____

_____

_____

_____

_____

_____

_____

_____

_____

_____

_____

_____

_____

_____

_____

_____

_____

MEDITATION 11

Psalm 127

God Provides

It is in vain that you rise up early and go late to rest, eating the bread of anxious toil; for He gives sleep to His beloved. v.2

Most of us experience some level of sleep deprivation in our lives, as parents, students, and/or because of our occupations. And most of us know the consequences – moodiness, anger, irritability, nervousness, fatigue, accident prone, physical problems and a slew of mental health problems that make medication necessary.

Unless God is behind the building and protecting our homes, city and nation, then all efforts are in vain – useless. No matter how many sleepless nights we are awake or half-sleep. Our human bodies need rest, and God provides for us during our sleep – healing and re-creating throughout the entire human body. God provides times of renewal – recreation in our lives.

Affirmation: I will rest.

Prayer: O LORD, help us to rest physically, mentally and spiritually.

Reflections / Notes

_____

_____

_____

_____

_____

_____

_____

_____

_____

_____

_____

_____

_____

_____

_____

_____

_____

_____

MEDITATION 12

Mark 12:38-44

Jesus Knows Your Giving Level

He (Jesus) sat down opposite the treasury, and watched the crowd putting money into the treasury. v.41a

I am reminded of what it can be like on disability. A steady check, yet very limited resources. I have learned to take the tithe right off the top of any monies I receive. Such giving has a promise attached to it – Malachi 3:8-12.

I have learned also to be a good steward with time, money and talent, so that everything is accounted for appropriately. Giving blindly is a sure way to promote all kinds of indiscretion on the part of givers and recipients. The church or organization that gives a weekly or quarterly accounting of gifts usually is entrusted with even more. Jesus knows your giving level of time, money and talent. Although we are told to encourage one another, God gives the ultimate reward.

Affirmation: I am a giver.

Prayer: O LORD, help me to be faithful to You in my giving. I am trusting You for provision.

Reflections / Notes

Meditation 13

1 Timothy 5:1-8

Respect

Do not speak harshly to an older man, but speak to him as to a father, to younger men as brothers, to older women as mothers, to younger women as sisters – with absolute purity. v.1-2

In all branches of the military, there are certain rankings. We know that these rankings dictate respect and behavior. The Bible also teaches us how to speak and respect one another in the human family. Sometimes those younger than elders, or within peer groups, can become impatient or frustrated, but the standard of respect is set Scripturally. This is our moral standard, dictated by the values and morals of the Scripture. It is in this way we maintain order in families, communities and whole societies.

Affirmation: I will respect myself and others.

Prayer: O LORD, empower us to treat others with dignity and respect.

Reflections / Notes

MEDITATION 14

1 Timothy 5:9-16

The Assistance of Relatives

If any believing man or woman has relatives who are really widows, let them assist then, let the church not be burdened, so that it can assist those who are real widows. v.16

When a person first becomes a widow, the church is there at the time of bereavement. As the realities of life set in on being sustained on a daily basis, there are family, the community of faith and friends who help out. Continued sustaining of those who are able to take care of themselves, is not healthy for the community or person. For those who are not capable or who have become disabled, the government provides money and care. Such government subsidies should not hinder relatives from providing care and comfort, and when necessary, some form of sustenance in hard economic times. Sometimes families cannot be as supportive as they would like, but may they always stay connected with emotional and psychological family support. We are warned in the Scriptures (Isaiah 58:6-14) not to turn our backs on our relatives and those in need.

Affirmation: I am there for my family and those in need.

Prayer: O LORD, link us to one another in ways that far outlive material wealth.

Reflections / Notes

MEDITATION 15

Luke 4:16-30

Prophets in the Ranks

There are different types of prophets: 1) Truth-tellers – One who states the reality of a situation; and 2) Foretellers – Those who predict the future. Sometimes one prophet can do both. Both types can usually find their grounding in the words of Scripture. Then there are true prophets and false prophets. Each is determined by whether their prophecy is fulfilled.

Those in the military have found it necessary to speak – vocally and through their writings. Military personnel and their families give voice to the realities of wartime and military mobilization(s). Each in their own way helps to set the policies and directions for the military and the country. Because we know what we know, we have capacity to bring healing and direction to our nation. We are not victors tossed about on the seas of time. We are men, women and families committed to our God and to our country in a common mission to serve God and country.

Affirmation: I am fulfilling my God given mission.

Prayer: O LORD, kingdoms rise and fall, empower us to be loyal to You, God of the Universe.

Reflections / Notes

MEDITATION 16

Psalm 113

Sunrise to Sunset

From the rising of the sun to its setting the name of the Lord is to be praised. The Lord is high above all nations, and His glory above the heavens. v. 3-4

No matter what is going on in our lives, the God of the Universe is still to be praised because God is God. No matter what human beings have decided by their free will and choice, God is still God. No matter our financial circumstances, no matter what our living quarters. No matter what our health or physical state…God is still God.

The God who cannot be contained by our human understanding is still God. God is not distant, but present at every life situation. God is with us on the mountaintop and in the valley; and all along life's journey. God is to be glorified in heaven and on earth. We are part of that process.

Let us praise and glorify the Lord.

Even when I don't feel like praising God, I do. I utter an Alleluia and Praise Your Holy Name. It is amazing how my spirit and continence changes. I can feel my chemistry changing.

Affirmation: I praise the LORD, Alleluia - seven (7) times or more, each day.

Prayer: O LORD, empower us to praise and glorify You. Thank You for lifting us each day of our lives.

31

Reflections / Notes

_____

_____

_____

_____

_____

_____

_____

_____

_____

_____

_____

_____

_____

_____

_____

_____

_____

MEDITATION 17

Psalm 94

God, My Keeper

If the Lord had not been my help, my soul would soon have lived in the land of silence. v.17

None of us is perfect. A loving God disciplines and chastises us, teaching us out of the Laws – Principles of God. He delivers us from the pit in many concrete ways. If you find yourself in a pit, call upon the living God that sees and hears all things, beyond the limits of any surveillance humans could ever devise.

Through the changes and chances of life, God is still a loving and forgiving God whose love holds us up when the cares of the heart are many. God meets us at the point of our need, bringing peace and comfort beyond what words can explain and the mind understands.

Affirmation: When the LORD gives me help, I will take it.

Prayer: O LORD, grant me the peace and strength that passes all understanding.

Reflections / Notes

MEDITATION 18

Deuteronomy 24:17-22

Drawing the Line

You shall not deprive a resident alien or an orphan of justice. v.17a

In the midst of refugees crossing into countries in unprecedented numbers, countries are dealing with security and economic issues, including high unemployment already existing in their countries. As children and adults continue to run for their lives from sure death situations, the people of God are moving to influence and enact laws and practices that will stabilize the refugee crisis and their economies.

What will a just comprehensive immigration policy look like? Our text in Deuteronomy gives us an indication of what may need to be considered.

As we seek safety and empowerment of ourselves, our families, friends and nation… how we treat immigrants may determine how God blesses **all** our undertakings.

Affirmation: Motto- 'On my honor I will do my duty to God and my country'.

Prayer: O LORD, help all in need of safety have it. Empower us to love You, ourselves and others in very practical ways.

Reflections / Notes

MEDITATION 19

Psalm 146

Trusting God

The Lord lifts up.....v.8b

Plans can change unexpectedly. You have plans for a trip or party, vacation, housewarming, school visitation and then there is 'a call-up.' Material possessions are packed or sold, or left behind in storage...if there is time. Insurance policies and wills are reviewed verbally or silently within your mind. Children are packed up, too, ready to say good-bye. They are leaving friends one more time. It can be like a whirlwind where you sometimes don't know where you will land.

God is with us in the whirlwind, calling us to lean on the LORD's presence. God is there to strengthen, to dry the tears and comfort the raw emotions. God moves through others. Beyond the orientation and training, we trust God to lift and deliver, and we work with God, our maker, to bring order and meaning out of chaos – the rough seas of our lives. Talking with Jesus, being in a relationship with Him, makes a difference.

Affirmation: I talk with Jesus every day.

Prayer: O Lord, thank You for being there.

Reflections / Notes

MEDITATION 20

---

1 Timothy 6:11-21

Making the Mark

Avoid the profane chatter and contradictions of what is falsely called knowledge; by professing it some have missed the mark as regards the faith. v. 20-21

Military families tend to know some things the general population does not know. We tend to move in silence and prayer, rehearsing thoughts only in our mind and hearts. We learn early there is a time to speak and time to keep silent.

Our LORD calls us away from profanity and the limited knowledge of human beings. God grants us the Holy Spirit's discernment, and leads us into a faith that cannot be manipulated by words or intent.

Affirmation: The Holy Spirit is increasing the gift of discernment in me.

Prayer: LORD God of the Universe, our Creator, Redeemer, and Sustainer, grant us Your discernment. Keep us from sick religion. Deliver us into the depths of Your Truth. Thank You.

Reflections / Notes

_____

_____

_____

_____

_____

_____

_____

_____

_____

_____

_____

_____

_____

_____

_____

_____

_____

MEDITATION 21

Colossians 2:6-15

Discernment and Power

See to it that no one takes you captive through philosophy and empty deceit, according to human tradition, according to the elemental spirits of the universe (or the rudiments of the world), and not according to Christ. v.8

The struggle not to be taken captive can be fierce. We must know the foundation of Truth, Forgiveness of sin, and Spiritual Birth and Resurrection in Christ. We must learn the tactics and strategies of the enemy of our souls – the demonic. Including the demonic taking on human form and functioning through human beings.

As we pray for ourselves and our families, let us pray and visually in our minds, see ourselves surrounded with the Light of Christ. (Close your eyes now and visualize being surrounded with the Light of Christ.)

Be strong in the Lord and the strength of His power. Put on the whole armor of God, spoken of in Ephesians 6:10-18.

Affirmation: I am not held captive to that which is not of God in Christ Jesus.

Prayer: O LORD, increase in us your wisdom and power.

Reflections / Notes

MEDITATION 22

Daniel 4:28-37

Today's Example – Nebuchadnezzar

When the period was over, I Nebuchadnezzar, lifted my eyes to heaven and my reason returned to me.v.34

Nebuchadnezzar was a ruler-king of the Kingdom of Babylon – the Babylonian Empire. He was a human being who came to believe he built his life and empire by his own power for his own glorification and majesty. He believed he was God. Basically, he became mentally ill and acted like an animal. It was not until he lifted up his eyes to heaven and blessed God, the most high – God of the Universe, and saw himself for who he was, that his sanity returned to him. When he came to the understanding that he was not the God of the Universe and spoke and acted accordingly, he was restored. His illness was only for a certain period of time, until he came to his senses – reason returned to him.

Affirmation: I worship the God of the Universe and keep my sanity.

Prayer: Our LORD, heal those who are mentally ill. May we always remember who you are and we belong to You. Help us to prevent such illnesses among us.

Reflections / Notes

MEDITATION 23

Hebrew 10:26-31

No Cheap Grace

How much worse punishment do you think will be deserved by those who have spurned the Son of God, profane the blood of the covenant by which they were sanctified, and outraged the Spirit of grace…? The Lord will judge His people.

The grace of God calls us to repentance and the changing of our behavior. Persistent sin leads to the chastisement of God. Sometimes people feel trapped into certain behaviors because of commitments that have been made. What do we do? People usually bite their tongue. Others pray for an opportunity to exit… a window of opportunity to open for them to exit. God hears and answers.

For some, after orientations and training, they realize things are not what they bargained for, especially after they realize the impact on their mind and core of being. Some wait it out and make the best of things. Others pray their way through and ask for healing and deliverance (without suicide). God answers.

Affirmation: I will live. I surrender my life and lives of my love ones into the hand of God.

Prayer: Thank you, Lord God, for hearing and answering us, and empowering us not to cheapen your grace.

Reflections / Notes

_____

_____

_____

_____

MEDITATION 24

Daniel 8:15-27

Dreams and Visions

When I, Daniel, had seen the vision, I tried to understand...Gabriel help this man understand the vision. v.15, 16

Dreams and visions and appearances of angels – celestial beings – are not uncommon when the Spirit of the Lord is poured out.

Sometimes dreams and visions are sent from God, and have meaning in the divine plan and purposes of God and the universe. Sometimes our dreams foretell and prepare us. Sometimes our dreams help us to process what has happened during the hours we are awake in our lives. Over time, one can learn to take control over dreams and flashbacks related to training and military service. Dreams then lose the power they once had to frighten and prevent you from functioning.

Dreams and visions, and the appearance of celestial beings, are not hallucinations, but you may need time (rest), nourishment, and sometimes medicine to recover from them.

Affirmation: I will come to know the meaning of my dreams.

Prayer: O LORD, help us to know when dreams and visions are from You and not coming from the inner recesses of our own minds and fears. Thank You for equipping and preparing us. Draw us close to You. Grant us peace.

Reflections / Notes

MEDITATION 25

Mark 13:1-8

Just the Beginning of Birth-pains

Many will come in my name saying I am…wars and rumors of wars do not be alarmed…nation will rise against nation, and kingdom against kingdom… earthquakes…famines.

This prophecy, given by Jesus the Christ, is timely at this point in history. It helps us to keep perspective on what time it is in the universe. We are living in a time when the Scriptures of many faiths are being fulfilled in our lifetime. Are you ready to deal with these "birth-pains?" Can we really ever be ready?

Jesus tells us these things so we will not be led astray by those who seek to divide and conquer us, or get us off-focus from what is important in life. We can do disaster management; we can prepare for global political upheaval without being their source, and stabilize our country as much as possible. Yes, we can be prepared for charlatans and spiritual pundits. We can even be prepared for war without starting one or being in one.

Affirmation: I am alert and discern the times I live in.

Prayer: O LORD, get us ready, keep us ready. Help us to stay faithful.

Reflections / Notes

MEDITATION 26

Psalm 13

God Delivers

But I trusted in your steadfast love; my heart shall rejoice in your salvation. v.5

How great and lasting is God's love. The seemingly smallest thing I pray for, God delivers. God delivers us from constant anxiety and fear, homelessness, addictions, confused thoughts, ignorance, and unemployment.

God delivers food to eat, shelter, and clothes to put on our bodies. These are all delivered sometimes through the work of our hands, and sometimes through the hands and thoughts of others.

God delivers us from our mistakes, giving us second chances most of the time. God delivers us from our sins and sinful nature through the obedience, death and resurrection of Jesus the Christ.

God places our sins in a sea of forgetfulness and remembers them no more. What a relief it is.

We continually experience the salvation of our God.

Affirmation: I trust in God's steadfast love.

Prayer: LORD, may I rejoice daily in Your salvation.

Reflections / Notes

_____

_____

_____

_____

_____

_____

_____

_____

_____

_____

_____

_____

_____

_____

_____

_____

_____

_____

MEDITATION 27

Hebrews 10:32-39

Endurance

For you need endurance, so that when you have done the will of God, you may receive what was promised. v. 36

As an athlete practices stretches each day – rain or shine, through all kinds of weather - so we as Christians are stretched in our faith through all kinds of life circumstances. At each moment in our journey, as we keep our faith in God, we also rest in the confidence that God has 'got us'. God has our back. And the peace that passes all understanding keeps our heart and mind in Christ Jesus, the author and finisher of our faith.

We keep holding on to the hand of God, sometimes encouraged by the presence of others to keep on keeping on, knowing our ultimate reward is sure. Hold on to the hand of God.

Affirmation: I do what I believe is the will of God.

Prayer: O LORD, help us to keep on living the faith we have in You.

Reflections / Notes

MEDITATION 28

Daniel 8:1-14

Vision of Destructive Power

It cast down truth to the ground and kept prospering in what it did.
v.12b

As houses of faith are trampled, bombed or burned around the world, and the truth is twisted or thrown away...taken from the light stand and thrust upon the ground to be trodden underfoot... when evil seems to prosper continually... we may ask – Is this the end of time? Can we turn things around? God only knows...and we remember that with God, nothing is impossible.

And so we keep our faith in God and step forth in our daily lives, to be used and empowered by a Mighty God for whom nothing is impossible.

Affirmation: I partner with God who makes all things possible.

Prayer: O LORD, empower us in a mighty way, in this hour of the universe.

Reflections / Notes

MEDITATION 29

Hebrews 10:11-14 (15-18) 19-25

Keep the Faith

...I will put my laws in their hearts, and I will write them on their minds... I will remember their sins and their lawless deeds no more. v.16c-17

Let us hold fast to the confession of our hope without wavering, for He who has promised is faithful.v.23

When Christ had offered for all time a single sacrifice for sins, He sat down at the right hand of God, and since then has been waiting "until his enemies would be made a footstool for his feet". v.12-13

Affirmation: I hold to my faith and encourage others to do the same.

Prayer: Amen and Amen. Come Lord Jesus.

Reflections / Notes

MEDITATION 30

Acts 7:54-8:1a

Persecution Then and Now

While they were stoning Stephen, he prayed, "Lord Jesus, receive my spirit." v.59

Religious zealots were killing and persecuting Christians. In the state of Colorado USA, Christian young people have been killed at church and school for confessing Christ in the 21st century. In Syria, one of the oldest Christian communities on earth has been destroyed by religious zealots that some call heretics and maniacs. In Palestine, Christian schools have been desecrated by Israeli soldiers. Houses of faith are burning to the ground, in this country and around the globe. Houses of faith continue to be bombed.

While we try to live calm and consistent lives, we pray each day for the safety of children and adults in our own family. Each day we pray and entrust them into the hands of God, having done all God has empowered us to do.

Affirmation: I pray for believers in my country and around the world.

Prayer: LORD, we pray for believers everywhere that we may live at peace. Amen.

Reflections / Notes

MEDITATION 31

1 Corinthians 15:20-28

Keeping Perspective

For He (Jesus the Christ) must reign until He has put all His enemies under His feet. v.27

Nothing is higher than Jesus Christ with God the Father and Holy Spirit- No ruler, no authority or power in the earth or universe, no human, spiritual or any other being.

We who belong to Christ will also reign with Christ, beginning now, for the Kingdom of God is within you. Just imagine how much untapped potential we each have.

Affirmation: I will walk in the potential God in Christ has given me.

Prayer: LORD, empower us to live to the fullest in You.

Reflections / Notes

MEDITATION 32

John 3:31-36

Eternity

Whoever believes in the Son has eternal life. v.36

Eternity means forever and ever, without end.

As Christians, we believe that the spirit of those who are no longer here on earth with us, still live on and on – forever. And so at gravesides or memorial services, the clergy person says, "rest in peace" – cease your activity in the earth realm and find your rest in God.

We are told in the New Testament not to have conversations with familiar spirits – the spirits of family and friends – ancestors. We are to tell them to "depart and rest in peace, in Jesus name", while we tune into our relationship with Christ and take care things in the earth realm.

Affirmation: With the help of God, I take care of the unfinished business that is here on earth to complete.

Prayer: O LORD, thank You for eternal rest. May we on earth take care of unfinished business according to your way and will.

Reflections / Notes

MEDITATION 33

Revelation 1:4b-8

Living Forever

"I am the Alpha and the Omega", says the Lord God, who is and who was and who is to come, the Almighty. v.8

The Lord God says I am the Beginning and the End.

Before time existed as we know and measure it, the Lord God Almighty existed. God's beginning has no human definition, although we know that God created in the beginning of time for the planet earth.

God's existence is beyond the end that we call judgment day. Indeed, God's kingdom and reign has no end, for God reigns forever and ever. God's dominion lasts forever.

The Almighty's reign begins in each of our hearts, minds and lives now and continues throughout eternity.

Affirmation: God is with me at all times.

Prayer: O LORD, thank You for beginning a good work in me, and bringing it to completion.

Reflections / Notes

MEDITATION 34

John 18:33-37

Knowing the Truth

Everyone who belongs to the truth listens to My voice. v.37c

For some, truth is relative – there is no absolute truth. Yet God gives each of us the Holy Spirit that helps us each to hear and discern what is the truth.

How do you know when something is true? You will know in your inner being as you reflect on what you hear, your experience and the Scriptures. Once you connect with truth, you will not bend to peer pressure that is wrong without mental, physical, spiritual, and emotional discomfort.

Sometimes we have been doing the "group thing" so long that we find ourselves disconnected from the Divine within us. We may call good evil, and evil good (Isaiah 5: 20). The call to each of us today is to reconnect more to the Divine, the Holy. This connection will be what helps us to clarify our values and to stand.

Affirmation: I am connected with God today. I read scripture, pray and live the Christian life every day.

Prayer: O LORD, thank You for connecting with us. Lift us to the place of Your Truth. Surround us with Your Holy Light. Thank You for empowering us to stand and move and live. Thank You.

Reflections / Notes

MEDITATION 35

Daniel 7:9-10, 13-14

The Kingdoms of Earth Rise and Fall

Earthly kings, presidents and governments have risen and fallen throughout history, and will continue to the end of earthly time as we have known it. Scriptures tell us to pray for governments and those in authority over us, so that we may live peaceful lives.

Today, we are encouraged to pray for the temporary authorities and governments in our life. Pray for elected and appointed officials, and all who work under them. Pray for law enforcement and justice systems. Pray for the military and all the lives they touch. Pray for government departments to function for the common good of all people.

Affirmation: I shape authorities and governments through prayer, communicating and action.

Prayer: O LORD, keep our government leaders open to the leading of Your voice and movement. Give special insight and wisdom. Bring them closer to You.

Reflections / Notes

_____

_____

_____

_____

_____

_____

_____

_____

_____

_____

_____

_____

_____

_____

_____

_____

_____

_____

_____

MEDITATION 36

John 16:25-33

Straight To the Father

On that day you will ask in my name. I do not say to you I will ask the Father on your behalf. v.26a

Jesus' disciples have direct access to the God of the Universe - Creator of heaven and earth, the Wisdom and Power of God.

Just as we as children had direct access to those who cared for us, so we have direct access to God. We go to the Father with our praise and thanksgiving. We talk to God about the little and big matters of our lives. We draw near to God during the ups and downs - through the mountain top and valley experiences of life. God hears us and speaks to us in our hearts, through Scripture, through others and through life circumstances. God is present, and uses you and me in the ordinary situations of our lives.

Affirmation: I listen to the Spirit within me that is in sync with my Creator, Redeemer and Sustainer.

Prayer: O LORD, thank You for being there. May I recognize You in the ordinary situations of my life.

Reflections / Notes

MEDITATION 37

Revelation 11:15-19

Who's In Charge?

"We give you thanks, Lord God Almighty, who are and who were, for you have taken your great power and begun to reign." v.17

A child learns very quickly who is in charge at home, at grandma's and grandpa's, and at school. As we grow older, we deal with supervisors and bosses, clients and colleagues. We come to know about military people, policemen, firefighters, emergency medical personnel, and doctors and nurses, religious leaders and others.

We also learn to take responsibility for our actions. As Christians, we learn that ultimately we are responsible to God, and that the final word is pronounced by the Lord, God Almighty.

Affirmation: Jesus the Christ is my LORD and Savior.

Prayer: O LORD, help me to only worship You. May You be the only God in my life.

Reflections / Notes

MEDITATION 38

Matthew 5:27-36

What's the Problem?

Everyone who looks at a woman (or man) with lust has already committed adultery with her (or him) in his (or her) heart. v.28

Choosing what you listen to and look at, are two of the keys to maintaining your Christian walk. Even what you wear is an indicator of your Christian walk.

Pornography is like an addiction. One way to stop the emotions, thoughts, longings and urges is to stop listening and looking. Stop the conversation – walk away, turn it off.

Asking God to empower you to stop and bring your thoughts and behaviors in line with the WORD (Scripture) are strategic keys. Through the Spirit of God working in your life, you can bring all thoughts and behavior into submission.

Affirmation: I can do all things through Christ who strengthens me.

Prayer: Help us, O LORD, to let our sexuality develop in a way that glorifies you and fulfills our needs for love, commitment and the continuance of life on earth.

Reflections / Notes

_____

_____

_____

_____

_____

_____

_____

_____

_____

_____

_____

_____

_____

_____

_____

_____

_____

_____

_____

MEDITATION 39

Psalm 55:1-23

Break Time – Enemies in Your House

Cast your burden on the LORD, and He will sustain you; He will never permit the righteous to be moved. v.22

Sometimes when you're uncertain about the mental state of someone you live with, there can be a continuous uneasiness. You are always on alert. The alert can be high or low, but it is always there. Such tension or stress wears on the body, mind and spirit.

Asking God to surround you with guardian angels and surround you with Holy Light eases the stress. Asking God to calm and protect love ones, and to bring order and healing is our cry.

Go outside. Enjoy the break time. Take a deep breath. Exhale and inhale. If you need to cry, then cry. Drink plenty of water to wash out toxins. Eat nutritious food. Take minerals and vitamins. Talk with someone. Physically exercise, walk if you are able – it does wonders. Do something social – with other people, or be around others. Go to prayer meeting or Bible study. Don't isolate yourself.

The trauma of the one you love, is your trauma too – only to a different degree.

Affirmation: I call upon the LORD, for the LORD saves me. v.16

Prayer: LORD, thank You for Your daily saving power.

Reflections / Notes

MEDITATION 40

Mark 10:17-31

Possessions

When he heard this, he was shocked and went away grieving for he had many possessions. v.22

When you have to move on a moment's notice – whether it is 2 weeks or 3 months' notice- packing up one's possessions each time you move can be a time for letting go, not only of some material possessions, but also some relationships.

As human beings, we grieve each loss and during each change. Moving, changing, letting go takes its toll on both adults and children. Stabilizing the environment in the midst of change at times can be a challenge. We thank God for always being present no matter what the situation; and wrapping us in spiritual arms and physical arms of family and friends.

Letting go and depending on a loving God can seem foolish and daunting. The key is holding onto God in the midst of change and loss, and knowing that God will make a way for every need to be met through you and others. The peace comes from knowing God is with you no matter what you're experiencing. With or without possessions, you have Jesus. God never lets go.

Affirmation: God is holding onto me.

Prayer: O Lord, thank you for being with me. Grant me the peace that passes all understanding.

Reflections / Notes

MEDITATION 41

Psalm 39

Wisdom and Forgiveness

"And now, O Lord, what do I wait for? My hope is in You. v.7

No one's life is perfect. All of us make mistakes. We think thoughts that may not be the most loving. We say something that we later wish we could take back; or don't say anything and then regret the fact that we didn't say anything. We hope and pray for second chances. Most times, we get our second chance; sometimes we do not get another chance. What's done is done.

The only being in the universe that gives unlimited forgiveness is God Almighty.

As we connect with God in Jesus Christ, we experience forgiveness in our personal lives. With the strength from our relationship with our God, we are able to forgive ourselves and others, and move on.

Affirmation: My hope is in You, O Lord. Your mercies are new every morning. Alleluia.

Prayer: Thank you, LORD, for being my hope and my strength. Give me wisdom. Empower me with Your Holy Spirit.

Reflections / Notes

MEDITATION 42

Hebrews 3:17-19

Help My Unbelief

So they were unable to enter because of unbelief. v.19

Can you imagine walking around in a wilderness for 40 years, when your final destination is in walking distance…a few steps away? Can you imagine driving or cycling and being lost, when all you had to do was believe the directions you received from someone? Instead of an hour or more, you could have been at your destination in 30 minutes or less. Can you imagine always being on the go, stopping to rest but never really resting, knowing you have not reached your destination yet?

In the Christian faith, believers find their rest by believing and trusting that Jesus Christ has died for our sins. We believe it and find relief from guilt and anxiety. We believe God, our ever present friend, so we are never truly alone.

Affirmation: I am obedient to the Living God. I believe what God has said and done in His Word. I have rest. I am resting in the arms of Jesus. (Close your eyes and imagine yourself resting in the arms of Jesus).

Prayer: Thank You for rest, O God, each day. Thank You for Your Holy Spirit that helps me to understand all Scripture and gives me wisdom and insight. Thank You for freeing me from sin, so I can be obedient to God. Thank You for empowering me to follow the directions of Scripture, making destination sure, and life journey filled with rest - like resting in the arms of Jesus.

Reflections / Notes

MEDITATION 43

Psalm 90:12-17

Counting Days

So teach us to count our days that we may gain a wise heart. v.17

We want to live long enough for our lives to have an impact on others, and to enjoy our family and friends. Most of us want to see our children, grandchildren and great grandchildren come into the world and prosper.

We count our days for a number of different reasons. We count the days until projects are done. If we are away from home, we count the days till we or a loved one will be home. We count the days till school starts, and the number of days till we receive a degree or certificate or discharge. We count vacation days. We count the days of our lives. In the midst of our counting, we want God to bless us, to prosper our work. We pray for the favor of God.

Affirmation: I count my days and have a wise heart.

Prayer: O LORD, thank you for Your wisdom. Let Your favor be upon me. Thank You.

Reflections / Notes

_____

_____

_____

_____

_____

_____

_____

_____

_____

_____

_____

_____

_____

_____

_____

_____

_____

MEDITATION 44

Matthew 15:1-9

Heart Check

All human precepts are not necessarily consistent with the principles, values and teachings of our Lord and Savior, Jesus the Christ.

What may be acceptable at the office or in the field may conflict with one's faith. Ultimately, we end up with a values conflict and realize our human precepts – principles, fall short of navigating the world God's way.

Sometimes we push this value conflict to the back shelf. Gradually we move farther and farther away from our relationship with God... something or someone else has taken the throne of our hearts. Gradually we become numb and then one day, we realize we are not in a relationship with God like we used to be or even want to be. At that point, God reminds us that He has never left us.

Affirmation: I honor God with my entire being.

Prayer: Help me, God. Draw my heart and being to You. Heal me. Make me consistent. Empower me to be Your disciple.

Reflections / Notes

MEDITATION 45

Hebrews 4:12-16

Nothing Hidden

Indeed, the Word of God is living and active....v.12

God's eyes are more searching, penetrating and accurate than any government surveillance system ever could be anywhere. Indeed, there are some things that only can be exposed by a loving God.

Ultimately, God is our judge, judging our thoughts and intentions of the heart, separating soul from spirit and tissues of our being. Isn't it great that it is a loving God that has this type of capacity to whom we must give ultimate account.

Indeed it is better to be in the hands of God, than in the hands of men.

Affirmation: I am in the hands of God.

Prayer: O LORD, help me to see me as You see me. Grant me insight, wisdom, love and peace.

Reflections / Notes

MEDITATION 46

Obadiah 1-9

Proud Hearts

Having confidence you can complete a task is important. Without some form of confidence, very little would get done. The type of pride that leads to downfall is what in the English language would be called arrogance. A haughtiness that brags about what it can be and do, leads to sure destruction.

If we talk too much about ourselves, lifting ourselves above others, "turning our noses up," even to the point of saying, "Who will bring me down to the ground?" The Lord reminds us that He can bring us down.

Affirmation: My confidence is in the Lord. I am not consumed with arrogance.

Prayer: LORD, help me stand, and never be brought down because of arrogance.

Reflections / Notes

MEDITATION 47

Obadiah 10-16

Boasting and Calamity

We are warned in Scripture not to gloat over the downfall of another human being, lest the same calamity come upon you. As a military family member, sometimes it is difficult not to cheer the victory and gloat over "the enemy."

Pats on the back and hugs – embracing that the battle – the task, the job, is over are well deserved and appropriate. Such achievements should be acknowledged. On the battlefront and at home, sometimes just making it through the day is an achievement.

Affirmation: I will encourage myself and others each day. With God's help, I will make it through the day and this season of life.

Prayer: Keep calamity far from me and those I love. Place encouraging arms around us throughout life's journey.

Reflections / Notes

MEDITATION 48

Obadiah 17-21

Mount Zion

What is Mount Zion? Where is Mount Zion? Who dwells in Mount Zion? Mount Zion is the highest place of ascent – the highest height. Some have tried to make it a physical place. Throughout the history of Israel, this has been done. It has been described as a specific location. As Christians, we believe it is the place where God and a believer are in fellowship. It could be your prayer and worship time. It can be the gathering with other believers to praise and worship God. It is a spiritual place where the living water of the Holy Spirit of God flows – giving life to all.

God gives each of us the breath of life each day. When we enter His presence with praise and worship, we deepen our relationship with the loving God and we go from one degree of glory to the next.

Affirmation: I am deepening my relationship with God. I read the Scripture and worship God. I spend time each day just praising God for being God.

Prayer: O LORD, help me to ascend to Mount Zion each day of my life.

Reflections / Notes

MEDITATION 49

Psalm 104:1-9, 24, 35b

God: Creator and Provider

Bless the Lord, O my soul. Praise the Lord! v.35b

God is awesome. God is so magnificent.

No matter where you are, imagine what original creation must have been like – the water, oceans, lakes and streams and all the fish and living things, both small and huge. Sit back and think about the mountains and volcanoes and glaciers; the moon and sun, and other stars and galaxies. Can you just see the lions and bears, all the plant and animal life; and human beings.

What a Creator and Provider God is - making sure everything is taken care of properly from sunrise to sunset. As caretakers, we have a lot of responsibility as we work with God.

Affirmation: I am working with the God of all creation.

Prayer: O Lord, thank You for Your creation. Empower me with Your Holy Spirit to be a good caretaker.

Reflections / Notes

MEDITATION 50

Hebrews 5:1-10

Being Appointed

And one does not presume to take this honor, but takes it only when called by God, just as Aaron was... v.4

During life, there are times when one volunteers or experiences what it is like to be appointed. The volunteerism turns into being selected – and all that comes to mean. You may ask yourself at some point, "How did I get myself into this?" or say, "This is not what I bargained for." But depending on the commitment you have made, or the papers you have signed, you decide to 'wait it out' and 'make the best of things.'

Sometimes we end up in places God never intended for us to be, experiencing things God did not want for us.

And so, I have learned to pray before I volunteer or accept the appointment. I literally ask God, and then maybe talk it over with family or close friends, so things can be put in perspective. If I believe it is an assignment given by God...I take it; if not, I let it go and trust God will make a way for me.

Affirmation: I talk to God before I talk to another human being. Deep within my heart and soul and mind God speaks to me. I will learn to accurately discern the voice of God.

Prayer: LORD, empower me with Your Holy Spirit to say what You want me to say, be what You want me to be, and go where You want me to go.

Reflections / Notes

Revelation 17:1-18

The Lamb as Conqueror

...the Lamb will conquer them, for He is Lord of lords and king of kings, and these with him are called and chosen and faithful. v.14

A great turning of the masses of people and nations to God is foretold in the Scriptures. How and when it will happen is not clear. We are told that at some point in time, every knee will bend and every tongue make confession that Jesus Christ is Lord.

As Christians, our goal is to live as kingdom of God people, beginning now and into eternity. Living our ordinary faith lives in our personal and public affairs will help to usher in the kingdom day by day on the earth.

Affirmation: With Christ, I am called, chosen and faithful. I am a conqueror.

Prayer: Empower me through the working of Your Holy Spirit to always choose Your way, O LORD, and to be faithful.

Reflections / Notes

MEDITATION 52

Mark 10:35-45

Greatness and Servanthood

Whoever wishes to be great among you must be your servant... v.44

Our lessons of servant hood are learned throughout life. Caring for children, spouse, parents, family, friends and neighbors leads to the lifting up of their voices and society to praise us as great. Being there for friends and comrades can lead to all kinds of accolades and medals being given to you.

In reality, being a servant is not easy. It requires being alert to the needs and desires of others. It can put a lot of wear and tear on one, physically, emotionally, mentally and spiritually. And at the end of the day- the mission, you are ready to drop from fatigue and get revitalized – refreshed. Times of refreshing are important for the human frame. It will help you go from better to great. Take the time.

Affirmation: I serve and I refresh myself.

Prayer: LORD, develop in me the life of a servant and provide me with deep refreshing along the journey of life.

Reflections / Notes

MEDITATION 53

Hebrews 6:1-12

Holding On

...so that you may not become sluggish, but imitators of those who through faith and patience inherit the promises. v.12

According to tradition, it is thought that James, the brother of Jesus, wrote the Book of Hebrews. He encourages us to "hold on" for our work will not be overlooked; and the love we show to others will be remembered.

As life in the world pulls at us and may cause some to fall away from the faith, James encourages us to hold fast to our faith. We hold fast by praying and meditating on Scriptures daily and following the Scriptures in our daily lives. To sum it all up, you hold fast by loving God and loving neighbor as yourself.

In the midst of competition, rising and falling stock prices, devaluation of the dollar, safety and health concerns, employment issues, the flowing of alcohol and drugs around us, God says, "hold on." " You will experience the fulfillment of My promises".

Affirmation: I believe what God has promised, God delivers.

Prayer: Lord, thanks for holding on to me (us). Forgive me (us) when I (we) stray. Bring me (us) back to You through the working of Your Holy Spirit.

Reflections / Notes

MEDITATION 54

Hebrews 6:13-20

Certainty of God's Promise

We have this hope, a pure and steadfast anchor of the soul. v.19b

> "Though the storms keep on raging in my life
> And sometimes, it's hard to tell the night from day
> Still this hope that lies within is reassured
> My soul is anchored,
> Is anchored in the Lord."
> – Douglas Miller

Affirmation: I am anchored in the LORD.

Prayer: Continue to anchor me in You, O LORD. Thank You.

Reflections / Notes

MEDITATION 55

John 13:1-17

Betraying Jesus

The devil had already put it into the heart of Judas, son of Simon Iscariot, to betray him. v.2

Can you imagine washing the feet and eating with someone who is about to betray you, or in thought, has already betrayed you? It's enough to make you distance yourself immediately – walk away, end any form of relationship that is left.

You may find yourself, day and night, trying to pick up the pieces.

People betray one another in a variety of ways. Some betray for a few pieces of silver – money, some for privilege and position, some for safety and survival.

What is important is that Jesus forgives the betrayer and helps us to forgive as well. Where the relationship with the betrayer ends up is left to you and me. God grants us wisdom in such decisions, and is with us either way to pick up the pieces of our broken hearts and lives.

Affirmation: I will live and not die. God helps me to get it right.

Prayer: O LORD, help me heal from and overcome disappointments and set-backs.

Reflections / Notes

MEDITATION 56

Psalm 75

The Wondrous Deeds of God

...but it is God who executes judgment, putting down one and lifting up another. v.7 At the set time that I appoint, I will judge with equity. v.2

At the set time, God will judge with fairness. No human court can match His justice. God is thorough.

Without His mercy, who would be able to remain standing? Thank God we have Jesus the Christ who died for our sins, our mistakes, violations of our relationship with God and others.

Thank God, that as when experience the beginning of His judgment – the conviction we feel in our conscience and heart, we are not destroyed. Though we may live with some of the ramifications of our behavior, God shows us mercy and helps us to forgive ourselves. As we repent, God brings newness of life each day and empowers us to live differently.

Affirmation: I will give God thanks for God's deeds in my life and the lives of others.

Prayer: Thank you, LORD God, for Your wondrous deeds. Praise You, O LORD, from the rising of the sun to the setting of the sun. You are God, there is no other, and You are worthy to be praised. Alleluia! Because You are God, no matter what is happening in our lives. Alleluia!

Reflections / Notes

MEDITATION 57

Psalm 91:9-16

A Prayer and An Answer

When they call me, I will answer them...v.15

After my sister had her first child, I taught Psalm 91 to my sister. She, in turn, taught it to her daughter, who memorized it as a little girl.

Believing Psalm 91 chases away fear and anxiety. It opens you up to receive the wisdom of God and energy of the Holy Spirit to move through life.

Verse 1. You_____(put your name there)

Verse 3. For He will deliver_____(put your name there)

Verse 4. He will cover _____(put your name there) with His pinions

Place your name throughout the Psalm. Close your eyes. Let each verse sink into your being.

Affirmation: When I call to God, God answers me. When we call to God, God answers us.

Prayer: O Lord, thank You for Your support and protection. Help me to stay under your protection, which is far better than human protection without you.

Reflections / Notes

MEDITATION 58

Mark 8:22-26

Alone With Jesus

He took the blind man by the hand and led him out of the village. v.23

Throughout our lives, we may live in several types of villages. As a military family, you may move from village to village and make a home in several different places.

Jesus takes your hand and takes you to a place where it's just you and him - away from the talk of others. He takes you to a place where it's just you and him - away from television, computers and mobile devices. A place where such things are turned off and you can hear His voice and experience the energy and healing only He can bring each of us. Take the time to sit quietly.

Ask God to minister to your spirit. When you read Your Bible, ask God to show and teach you what He wants you to learn at that point in time. God will.

Affirmation: Alone with Jesus, I am energized to new beginnings. I take the time. I am energized. I move into new beginnings each day.

Prayer: O LORD, speak to me, touch me. Raise me up each day to experience new beginnings.

Reflections / Notes

MEDITATION 59

Mark 10:46-52

Giving Sight to the Blind

Many sternly ordered him to be quiet, but he cried out even more loudly, "Son of David, have mercy on me!" v.47

The healing begins with the first thought. In the calling out, the blind Bartimaeus begins to move toward His healing. He begins to move toward the possibilities of experiencing life differently – of seeing. His faith had been ignited. Perhaps he had heard about this Jesus of Nazareth from over-hearing the talk of others. Perhaps he had been told about him. He heard and now is his opportunity to be touched by Jesus. He does not want to miss it. He will not let the crowd or those around him silence him. He cries out, calling Jesus by His ancestral link, calling out for mercy, calling out in hope. And Jesus responds.

Sometimes we get exactly what we ask for in the physical realm. We know that God is always at work in the spiritual realm, drawing us closer to him. Then it happens, we experience in the physical concrete world what we have prayed for in our hearts, minds and souls.

Affirmation: I am drawing closer and closer to God and being healed and transformed in my body and spirit daily.

Prayer: Thank You, LORD, for the transforming power of Your Word and Spirit.

Reflections / Notes

_____

_____

_____

_____

_____

_____

_____

_____

_____

_____

_____

_____

_____

_____

_____

_____

_____

MEDITATION 60

Nehemiah 1:1-11

Knowing the Situation

...and I asked them...v.2b

Nehemiah did not let his imagination run wild, trying to figure out what was happening, what people were thinking and experiencing. He asked them. When he took the time to ask, he was able to get a true status of the situation.

Oftentimes we ask what is going on with our spouse or relative or child, who is in the military; or ask what he or she is thinking... and our love one is silent. Sometimes we, ourselves, are silent. No human being can get an accurate status check. .

I learned to speak with other families about some things, but I knew I could speak to God about

all things.

Away from everyone, I talk to God... not just in my mind silently, but verbally. God knows my thoughts and verbalized words. The time spent with God is never wasted. I rise with the confidence God Almighty has heard me and is responding. I am not alone.

Do you have a prayer language (speaking in tongues)? If not, pray to receive it. It will give rest to your mind and allow you to exhale and feel relief in your entire being.

Affirmation: The God who loves me hears every thought and spoken word, and knows what the Spirit says.

Prayer: O Lord, help me.. Pour out your Spirit upon me. Give me the gift of speaking in tongues (1 Cor. 12).

Reflections / Notes

MEDITATION 61

Psalm 34:1-8 (19-22)

Deliverance from Trouble

The Lord redeems the life of His servants; none of those who take refuge in him will be condemned. v.22

I sought the Lord, and He answered me; and delivered me from all my fears. v.4

God is a deliverer. We can have many fears. Many of us have learned over time to place our concerns into the hands of God. We come to accept that our loved one has made decisions about how he/she will live life. We may pray daily for safety and that life will be preserved, but we know they have made a decision to be placed in harm's way. No matter how noble, it is a decision that has been made.

So we release them into the care of God, working through us and others. God is in the delivering business. God delivers food on the table to eat, housing to live in, health care, jobs, college tuition. It is a package deal when you know the LORD, no matter what God-given assignment you serve in. God delivers physically, emotionally, mentally and spiritually-meeting the needs of the whole human being.

Affirmation: God delivers me.

Prayer: O LORD, thank You for Your deliverance.

Reflections / Notes

_____
_____
_____
_____
_____
_____
_____
_____
_____
_____
_____
_____

MEDITATION 62

Isaiah 59:9-19

God's Response to Injustice and Oppression

So those in the west shall fear the name of the Lord, and those in the east, His glory...in eternal matters. v.19

It is far safer to be on the side of God, than on the side of human beings that execute injustice and oppress other members of the human family.

It seems like anyone of us can be caught up in a multitude of injustices and oppressive acts.

As we pray to exit such behaviors as individuals, families, communities and a nation, we ask God to be merciful toward all. May God give us wisdom, insight and discernment to take the proper actions. May we have the power of the Spirit to act as instruments of God: breaking the bonds of oppression, speaking truth and executing justice.

Affirmation: I am an instrument of the Almighty God bringing love and justice to the earth.

Prayer: Empower me to be Your instrument, O LORD.

Reflections / Notes

_____

_____

_____

_____

_____

_____

_____

_____

_____

_____

_____

_____

_____

_____

_____

_____

_____

_____

MEDITATION 63

I Peter 2:1-10

Our Living Hope

Concerning this salvation, the prophets who prophesized of the grace that was to be yours made careful search and inquiry...v.10a

The grace of God is great to experience. To know that your sins - those things, that nature that separates us from God- have been forgiven and the slate wiped clean in your life, makes you shout – 'Alleluia, thank You, Jesus!'.

We pray that we and our loved ones, especially, experience this grace. This is the grace that reaches into every mind, house, bedroom, meeting place; and into the inner planning and implementation of every mission. May we not cheapen the grace God has extended to each of us. May each moment be filled with true repentance, strength for new beginnings, and allegiance to the living God.

Affirmation: I am growing and experiencing the grace of God through Jesus Christ. God's grace reaches into the depth of my mind, soul and heart. It strengthens me to live life to its fullest.

Prayer: Thank You for Your our grace, O LORD, may I never cheapen it.

Reflections / Notes

Psalm 28

Thanks Lord

Blessed be the Lord for He has heard the sound of my pleadings. v.6

Alleluia! Thank You, LORD.

Thank You for Your answers to my prayers.
Thank You for the food, and the clothing, and the shelter.
Thank You for the peace in my house.
Thank You for the strength.
Thank You for family and friends.
 Thank You for safe travel.
Thank You for Your presence.
Thank You for good doctors and medical care and all the equipment we
    need.
Thank You for benefits.
Thank You for the vehicle.
Thank You for the job, for your patience and endurance.
Thank You for wisdom.
Thank You for safety.

I Praise You and bless Your Holy Name. Alleluia!

Affirmation: God hears and answers my prayers.

Prayer: Thank You, LORD.

Reflections / Notes

MEDITATION 65

Psalm 119:17-24

Open My Eyes

Open my eyes, so that I may behold wonderous things out of your law.
v. 18

Going deeper into the Word of God can be exciting. The Scriptures have so many different shades of meaning. Even the numbers have meaning, as do places and names. Using study tools to delve deeper into the Bible is always helpful. At one point, even the Wall Street Journal was advertising study tools for understanding the Scriptures in their original languages. Those in the business world are also deepening their relationship with Jesus Christ.

God continues to open intellectual and spiritual eyes. Studying the Scriptures can be exciting. Now a days you have to make sure you have the real Scriptures. Counterfeits have been on the market for a while. But do not be discouraged. Places like the American Bible Society (which also has a version with the Vatican Seal), still sell Bibles at very reasonable costs and television ministries are also offering Bibles. As mentioned earlier, the Scriptures I am using are from the New Revised Standard Version, published by the Division of Christian Education of the National Council of Churches of Christ in the USA. As you explore the Scriptures, reliable sources are important.

Affirmation: God is opening my eyes to the meaning of Scripture.

Prayer: Thank You for opening my eyes LORD. Help me to get the most accurate copy of Your Word.

Reflections / Notes

MEDITATION 66

Jeremiah 33:1-11

Healing After Punishment

I am going to bring it recovery and healing... v.6a

There are some who say God is judging the nations, this country included. In the Scriptures, judgment always comes before the blessing of people. God in His mercy first sends teachers and prophets so the people know where they have fallen short. If the people do not repent, then punishment comes.

The child is first taught, and later is told where they have fallen short and punished, and then is hugged by the parent. As people of God and nations, we are first taught, then told where we have fallen short, punished, and then hugged by a loving God. When we repent, God brings some level of healing into our lives. We go through some level of recovery.

Great teaching is going out across this country and around the globe. Prophets (preachers) are calling people to repentance. Without the 180° turn-around by people, there is punishment- chastisement, which is different from persecution. May all of us pass from judgment into recovery and blessings, with the least amount of possible scars.

Affirmation: God loves me. God is teaching me. I am on the journey from judgment to blessings.

Prayer: LORD, thank You for Your mercy. Empower me by the inner working of Your Spirit. Thank You for Your love. Thank You for bringing us through. Bless me, my family, community and nation.

Reflections / Notes

MEDITATION 67

Romans 3:21-31

Redeemed

Since all have sinned and fall short of the glory of God; they are now justified by His grace, as a gift through the redemption that is in Christ Jesus, v.23-24

Praise God! We have all been saved because of what Christ has done for us. The sacrifice of Jesus the Christ and His resurrection means that we can connect with God and experience the spiritual power of the resurrection, beginning now and in its fullness in eternity. Jesus has redeemed my life, given me life, and connected me with a relationship with the living God of the Universe.

No one is perfect. We have all messed up in some way. But God's grace – unmerited mercy, is something that I could not make happen in my human strength. God's grace reaches to my lowest valley and my highest mountain of achievement, and saves me from myself. In Christ, the kingdom of God within me is ignited and connected to the living God. Christ in you is your hope of glory. You are redeemed.

Affirmation: I live experiencing the grace of God daily.

Prayer: Thank You, LORD, for Your grace. Thank You for Jesus.

Reflections / Notes

MEDITATION 68

Luke 10:25-37

Inheriting Eternal Life

... *"You shall love the Lord your God with all your heart, and with all your soul and with all your strength, and with all your mind; and your neighbor as yourself.*

Loving God is not easy. But after doing it for a while it becomes second nature. There can be a number of challenges in the world to making and keeping God as #1 in your life. Children, spouses, family, money, employment all can become our main focus. The key is to say "Lord, You are my Source; I am looking to you to go through the day dealing with my children, family, spouse, money, and/or job". "Empower me with your Spirit to do what I must do today." "Fill me with Your love". This keeps the loving God on the throne of one's life and each of us connected for daily direction and improvement.

As for loving your neighbor as yourself, pray: "LORD, please give me Your love so I can love my neighbor and myself correctly. Thank You."

Affirmation: I ask God and God answers. God is filling me with Divine love for myself and others.

Prayer: LORD, thank You for Your love and the Eternal Spring of Life that flows within and through me.

Reflections / Notes

Psalm 146

Praises for God's Help

Praise the Lord! Praise the Lord, O my soul. v.1

Praise the LORD! Praise the LORD, O my soul! I feel so much better. Thank You for helping me. Thank You for being there. Thank You for being God.

O what a relief it is to know the living God is with you. It takes the stress level down when you know the One True and Loving God is with you, no matter what you're going through.

In your mind, imagine yourself surrounded by Divine Light from head to toe. Wrap the Light around you like a cylinder. You'll feel the difference as you go through your day.

Affirmation: I am surrounded by the Light of Christ and I feel great.

Prayer: Praise the LORD, O my soul.

Reflections / Notes

MEDITATION 70

Hebrews 9:11-14

Nothing Like The Blood of Jesus

For if the blood of goats and bulls, with the sprinkling of the ashes of a heifer, sanctifies those who have been defiled so that their flesh is purified, how much more will the blood of Christ... v.13

The power of the blood of Jesus the Christ has been talked about by Christian believers for over 2,000 years. It is not magic. It is an incredible spiritual phenomenon. The blood of Jesus makes us holy and works within us, preparing and strengthening us into the passage of eternal life. Its action upon us and within us continues long after we take Holy Communion (the Lord's Supper). Working together with the Spirit of God, it brings newness of life to our mind, and peace that passes human understanding.

The blood of Jesus connects us to a covenant relationship with God the Father, Son, and Holy Spirit. It washes away our sin (covers our sin) so we are purified and can enter into discussion with a Holy God. The complete understanding of how it works is still a mystery. Its power is not to be taken lightly or mocked. Indeed, it is the power of God that brings salvation.

Affirmation: I will experience the sanctifying power of the Blood of Jesus to its fullness in my life.

Prayer: O God, we thank You for Your Son, Jesus the Christ, and all that He has done to unite us with You.

Reflections / Notes

MEDITATION 71

Proverbs 15:1-17

Impacting the Mood

A soft answer turns away wrath, but a harsh word stirs up anger. v.1

The tone of voice and words we use can produce chemical reactions in the brain that can effect mood and behavior, and even create new brain cells. All this can happen in a matter of seconds. Present day neuroscience is telling us what the sages of old who communicated the Scripture already told us. Scientists are just telling us how all this works.

Many of us know from relating to family members and others how to calm the angry person. We also know how words can put a person on the defense or can break a person's spirit, lead to tears or just the opposite – to laughter.

To bring down the tension in the house, speak in softer, loving words and tones. Playing nature music may help as well, especially music with water falls. You may also decide to take a walk or go to the gym. Taking a warm bath or dipping yourself up and down in a pool will help to wash away some of the tension, fatigue and emotional pain. To help an angry loved one, kicking a ball can help – keep everybody in the family playing kick-ball or some other physical activity. There are also exercises for the disabled. Ask a physical therapist.

Affirmation: I will speak words in tones that build-up the person. I will show my love in words and actions.

Prayer: Renew me, O Lord, as I participate in the renewing of the lives of others.

Reflections / Notes

MEDITATION 72

Proverbs 19:24-29

A Good Challenge

Reprove the intelligent, and they will gain knowledge. v.25b

Correct the intelligent and they will gain knowledge. Very few people resist correction so things can go better. The key is in how you say it. I try not to "put down" anyone. Good criticism starts out with a positive – a compliment. And then one might say, "Perhaps you would like to consider another way of doing this."

In the general population, telling people what to do in a non-teaching demeanor can prove difficult. In military families, people are used to following orders with limited discussion, if any. It is good to talk with one another, to share our thoughts and feelings. As we build relationships with our children, we try to instill discipline. In our society, we want our children to be able to think, so they are productive citizens, not given to following demagogues or those trends that can lead to anarchy. The task is not easy.

Affirmation: I give correction to my family and to those who have functioning intellect, so they may increase in knowledge, understanding and wisdom.

Prayer: LORD, give us the wisdom and courage to challenge one another, so we will grow in knowledge, understanding and wisdom. Thank You for giving me the words to say.

Reflections / Notes

MEDITATION 73

Proverbs 21:1-17

Values Clarification

All deeds are right in the sight of the doer, but the Lord weighs the heart. v.2

I am so glad that the Lord knows and weighs the heart with all its longings. Sometimes we do what we do because we're asked or told to do it. It is the routine. It is what is expected to do the job. It is protocol. But, we are not at our best. In our hearts, we know the truth, and what we would have liked to have done, if given the opportunity. Sometimes there are conflicts with one's deepest held values. Values that will not change and should not be changed by anyone. Take a deep breath, exhale and say, "God, help me."

God helps each of us get through those moments and empowers us through the working of the Holy Spirit to accept forgiveness, forgive ourselves and come into balance again. We long for the time of no values conflict, and God grants this to us. At some point, each of us will make the decision to balance and live the truth.

Affirmation: The LORD is working mightily in me.

Prayer: O Lord, thank You for Your peace.

Reflections / Notes

Meditation 74

Matthew 21:23-32

Ending Up Doing the Right Thing

...but later he changed is mind...v.29b

Someone invited you to dinner. You say you won't be able to make it, but thanks for the invite. After some thought, you change your mind and call and say you'll be there. The evening ends up being refreshing for you. You're glad you went. Being around other people gave you energy and helped you to remember there are others going through what you are, and will be supportive – you are not alone. It was a nice turn-out.

You may be asked to complete a task. At first, in your mind, you say, no thank you. You don't raise your hand or say anything. Later, you think about it and think maybe the right thing is to complete the task. You do. It ends up being a challenge to complete, but you are constantly in prayer as you work to finish the task.

In military life, there are ramifications to the decisions you make. You cannot be wishy-washy. You are expected to be forthright and dependable. Even the silence speaks.

Affirmation: I will do what I say I will do. I ask God to help me to follow through on my commitments. I 'count the cost' before saying yes.

Prayer: O LORD, help me "at the end of the day" to have done the right thing.

Reflections / Notes

MEDITATION 75

James 3:1-12

The Power of the Tongue

With it we bless the Lord and Father, and with it we curse those who are made in the likeness of God. v.9

With the tongue, one can shape his/her future and the future of others. With the tongue, we can spill out the negative-like poison and the words take on a life of their own. Truly the power of life and death is in the tongue....whether you are commander in chief, or a man and woman contemplating having children. Our words lead to chemical actions within us and actions in the world.

As Christians, we are connected with the source of all life and love. No matter how angry we become, no matter how hard, our goal is to think and speak words of life and love so we create and not destroy brain cells. Our goal is to promote health and not illness (mental or physical). We are to be co-creators with God, being transformed through the renewing of our thoughts (mind); and through our thoughts the changing of our cells to produce healthy bodies and minds.

Affirmation: I will speak the truth in love – I will speak life into the lives of others.

Prayer: O LORD, help me to speak the truth in love and to give life with my words.

Reflections / Notes

MEDITATION 76

Colossians 3:1-11

Raised

You have been raised with Christ...v.3a

Within each day there are moments when we are continually raised by God to our full stature with Christ. When we greet each other in love with a hug, or connect with one another through a phone call or electronic message, and have positive, uplifting words that build each other up, we rise. Having a friend or family member who calls every day and people to give you a safe hug is vital to healthy living and helps us to rise spiritually and as humane human beings.

Psychologists say two hugs a day can help us be psychologically, physically and spiritually well. A healthy human touch gives us energy. When we are believers, we know energy is from the Divine Source of all life and renews us daily.

Affirmation: I am raised in Christ.

Prayer: Thank You, LORD, for your Divine energy. Empower me to be all I can be as a Christian. Thank You for Your love and patience coming directly from You and through others.

Reflections / Notes

_____

_____

_____

_____

_____

_____

_____

_____

_____

_____

_____

_____

_____

_____

_____

_____

_____

MEDITATION 77

Romans 3:9-20

The Purpose of the Laws of God

There is nothing like knowing when you "blew" something. Mistakes get made. No matter how hard we try, we are not perfect. At some point, we come to rest in the fact that God forgives us; but forgiving ourselves can be a challenge. The mistake or sin can play like a recording over and over in one's mind, and one's heart can feel heavy. If we have offended a person, an apology may be in order and correcting of the wrong.

There comes a point eventually when you just have to let it go.

A good exercise is to write on a piece of paper what the offense is or was and place it on the ground and burn it, or flush it down the toilet.

No one is perfect. Take a deep breath. Exhale the mistake and inhale forgiveness. **Affirmation:** I am forgiven.

Prayer: LORD, thank you for your measuring rod and forgiveness. Empower me to be faithful to you.

Reflections / Notes

MEDITATION 78

Proverbs 29:1-27

Fear vs Trust

Many seek the favor of a ruler, but it is from the Lord that one gets justice. v.26

Human fear lays a snare, but one who trusts in the Lord is secure. v.26

Human fear can lead to all kinds of imaginations of the mind. It can lead us to perceptions that are not true. It can lead to poor judgment and faulty or erroneous decisions. Human fear can lead to mental disorders, such as anxiety, paranoia, depression, lengthened duration of PTSD and stress on the adrenal gland. The fears of another person can set in motion a whole scenario of events, whether one is dealing within you, your family, community or nation. Human fear can breed lies, panic, anger and violence (economic, social, and physical).

Trusting in God reduces fear and relieves the body of stresses causing imbalances that can affect the entire body.

Trusting God brings us back into the balance of spiritual, physical, and mental health. It brings calm and allows love to flow – healing body, mind, spirit and relationships.

Affirmation: I trust in the LORD and am secure. **Prayer:** I trust You Lord. Thank You.

Reflections / Notes

Psalm 73:21-28

No Matter What

Nevertheless I am continually with you; you hold my right hand. v.23

Another deployment…
Another move…
Another doctor visit…
Another job interview…
Another location to look for employment…
Another baby…
Another day without communication…
Another day of wondering and waiting…
Another review of the will and legal papers…
Another income issue…
Another concern over safety and mental status…
The need for another break…
Another delayed celebration…

In your mind, visualize yourself resting in the arms of Jesus. Take three deep breaths, and rest in His arms.

Affirmation: God is with me.

Prayer: Hold us close, LORD. Surround us and encourage us through the working of your Holy Spirit within us and through others.

Reflections / Notes

MEDITATION 80

---

1 Corinthians 2:1-5

Keep It Simple

...so that your faith might rest not on human wisdom but on the power of God. v.5

God keeps things very simple for us to understand and hold onto. The life, death and resurrection of Jesus the Christ is a simple story with magnificent results.

That God so loved the world that He gave His only Son as a living sacrifice for your sins. That God has forgiven each of us our sins, and empowers us with the Holy Spirit to live the Christian life is tremendous. That all this is uniting us with the God of the Universe and bringing us into our full stature of sons and daughters of the living God is a blessing beyond measure.

This is the story of the power of God to turn lives around and raise each of us up in spirit each day, now into eternity.

Affirmation: I am a child of the living God.

Prayer: Thank you for forgiving my sins and being with me every day.

Reflections / Notes

MEDITATION 81

Romans 11:25-32

How Long Do We Have?

...I want you to understand this mystery; a hardening has come upon part of Israel, until the full number of the Gentiles has come in. v.25

Well, one thing is for sure – we don't have forever for our entire family, community, nation and world to receive Jesus Christ as Lord and Savior. Once the "full number of Gentiles has come in," all Israel will be saved as well. In the meantime, we gather those we love and care about with us into the faith.

Intercessory prayer, and prayer and fasting are a must. Let us read and follow the Scriptures daily.

As we come together with others in the faith to praise and worship God, and encourage one another, let us always remember that we are linked to the God of the Universe, and with God, nothing is impossible.

Affirmation: I am in a relationship with the God of the Universe and we are working together.

Prayer: Thank you, O LORD, for bringing us into the community of the faithful.

Reflections / Notes

_____

_____

_____

_____

_____

_____

_____

_____

_____

_____

_____

_____

_____

_____

_____

_____

_____

_____

MEDITATION 82

Matthew 23:29-39

Pray for Clergy

Therefore I send you prophets, sages and scribes...v.34

Chaplains in the military are trained to minister to the human spirit and to support all things that will energize and support the human spirit of service people and their families. Most conversations may be specifically faith neutral, unless one is hired specifically as a Protestant, Muslim or Catholic chaplain, etc. Even then, you must know the basics of spirituality and what affects the human spirit and morale formation.

The trust factor between clergy, the military service person and their families can be eroded when clergy have to report on mental status that can affect a service person's tour of duty and future in the military service. Those serving make the decision when to speak to a chaplain or clergy person, who may be a better source for making spiritual sense of what is going on.

Praying for well-equipped, faith-filled clergy and mental health professional therapists is very important.

Affirmation: I will pray for faith-filled practicing clergy and other professionals in my life.

Prayer: O LORD, continue to raise up faith-filled clergy and professionals for the sustained healing and comforting of military and their families.

Reflections / Notes

_____

_____

_____

_____

_____

_____

_____

_____

_____

_____

_____

_____

_____

_____

_____

_____

_____

MEDITATION 83

Psalm 1

Renewal and Revival

....on His (the Lord's) law they meditate day and night. v2b

Meditating on the LORD's WORD - the Scriptures, during the day and at night brings direction and healing to body, mind and spirit. By reading, memorizing and reflecting on a verse or passage, the Word sinks in and becomes a part of one's being.

It is always good to keep verses in context of the entire chapter so we do not get lead astray in our understanding. Study tools are available in a number of Bibles nowadays – look for those done by Biblical Scholars and their affiliation, which are usually listed in the front of the volume.

It is good to memorize, so that as you go through the changes and chances of life, you can bring to mind Scriptures to hold onto for comfort, healing, encouragement and direction.

Affirmation: The Holy Spirit helps me make Scripture a part of my being.

Prayer: O LORD, thank You for Your daily revelation to me in the Scriptures.

Reflections / Notes

MEDITATION 84

James 3:13-4; 3, 7-8a

Drawing Near

Draw near to God and God will draw near to you. v.8a

How does one draw near to God? Some people do it by caring for and enjoying the environment – oceans, streams, rivers, sunrise and sunsets, hiking, farming, boating, flying, looking through a telescope, walking through forests, resting on beaches, experiencing deserts and mountains, walking or running. Others draw near to God through relationships with family and friends, celebrations – birthdays, anniversaries and holiday gatherings. Some draw near to God through private or communal prayer and worship. Some draw near to God by reading Scripture, experiencing the rituals of Baptism, laying on of hands and anointing with oil for healing, and/or the Lord's Supper. Some draw close to God at times of tragedy or during the "storms of life."

God draws us through the Spirit, throughout our life journey. We can ignore the pull. We can busy ourselves with a variety of things, or we can respond by being in relationship – talking with and falling in love with the will and ways of God daily.

The burden is a whole light lighter when you link up with Jesus.

Affirmation: I am connected to the God of the Universe alive in me and all creation.

Prayer: O LORD, thanks for being there.

Reflections / Notes

MEDITATION 85

Proverbs 27:1-27

Life

Do not boast about tomorrow, for you do not know what a day may bring. v.1

Things can change overnight, one decision, one phone call, one e-mail, or one text message can supersede all previous plans.

What you said you would do the next day is cancelled or postponed.

And so we learn to hold our plans close in a subdued emotional state so one does not go through an emotional roller coaster. You learn to go with the flow and do activities that counter the stress. Get together with friends and/or other family and friends. Call a trusted confidant and talk. Exercise – go for a walk. Do last-minute things together and give plenty of hugs…

And all the while, you say your prayers, and remain as calm as possible so disappointment and frustration does not show through in their intensity.

In your mind visually imagine, you resting your whole body in the arms of Jesus, take three deep breaths and rest against His chest and become relaxed and comforted.

Affirmation: I am flexible and able to recalibrate.

Prayer: Thank You, LORD, for being with me, strengthening me and giving me wisdom and peace during the changes and chances of life.

Reflections / Notes

MEDITATION 86

James 4:8-17

Maintaining Integrity

Instead you ought to say, "If the Lord wishes, we will live and do this or that." v.15

Truth be told, none of us really knows for sure what the future holds – no matter what thoughts we think, no matter how much positive thinking we do, no matter what plans we make.

Praying at the beginning of each day, we ask God to anoint our minds and heart to think and do what is in line with God's wishes – God's will. Following the Scriptures – we number our days...putting things in perspective. We pause and worship God. We seek Godly counsel. We build up our houses – families and shelter, we provide for our household. We lay up wealth for our children. We do our best not to procrastinate, for the seasons of God and life change. And we remember that human beings do not have the final say, the God of the Universe does.

Affirmation: I will stay in communication with God and walk in what I believe is God's will.

Prayer: O LORD, reveal your will to me and comfort me through your Scriptures.

Reflections / Notes

172

MEDITATION 87

Ecclesiastes 4:9-16

No Lone Rangers

"Two are better than one, because they have a good reward for their toil. For if they fall, one will lift up the other, but woe to one who is alone and falls and does not have another to help. v.9-10

As human beings, we need one another. None of us is meant to be alone in life. Sociologists and psychologists say we are social beings – we need to connect with other human beings in order to be healthy and survive. For this reason there are families and friends, support groups, faith gatherings, teams, clubs and associations. All hopefully helping us to fulfill our potential, and being there through life's journey.

Affirmation: I connect with other human beings daily. I am not isolated by myself.

Prayer: Thank You LORD for never leaving me alone. Thank You for family and friends along life's journey.

Reflections / Notes

James 5:1-6

The Cries of the Harvesters

...the cries of the harvesters have reached the ears of the Lord of hosts. v.4c

As some farmlands across the nation experience flooding or drought, many are asking why is God allowing this to happen to us. A season of reflection is taking place.

Questions we could ask are: Are we treating creation and its fruits properly? Are harvesters being paid just wages and treated properly?

Other than climatic conditions being the result of the activities of human beings, we need to ask God to give us understanding. We need to ask God to empower us to act, so no one goes hungry, and harvesters are treated justly by their employers and this nation. Then our children and their descendants will be able to live on the planet earth until the end of time when Jesus comes.

Affirmation: I am a good steward of creation.

Prayer: O Lord, we thank You for Your creation and all its wildlife and fruits. We thank you for the fish of the sea and birds of the air, and all creatures upon the earth. Give us wisdom in caring for your creation. May we be a just and loving nation to all who live here.

Reflections / Notes

MEDITATION 89

Psalm 54

God's Human Assistants

But surely, God is my helper, the Lord is with those who uphold my life. v.4

Most of us can make a list of those we believed were sent by God to be in our lives to help us get through life. The list would include those who assists us with tasks and transitions, those who go to bat for and with us- being there along the way. God can use all kinds of people.

Take some time now and in your mind reflect back on those people and the circumstances which brought them into your life. You may want to write down who they were and what they did. Some people's names you will know, and perhaps some names you will never know. Most of us could probably write a book about the people God sent as Human Assistants.

I believe some of us will write that book of gratitude and thanksgiving.

Affirmation: God is my helper.

Prayer: LORD, thank you for sending your human assistants into my life. Please bless them in a special way.

Reflections / Notes

MEDITATION 90

Acts 4:13-31

The Importance of the Response of People

After threatening them again, they let them go, finding no way to punish them because of the people, for all of them praised God for what had happened. v.21

The response of people always matters in the decision-making process. Even when channels of communication are very structured and restrictive, the human response is very important and eventually is taken into consideration in some way. It matters, even when you are 'sucking up,' your emotions. Even that response will have an impact upon your body and can lead to emotional numbing, poor communication, outbursts of uncontrollable anger, domestic violence, physical illness, addictions, silence, depression and suicide.

As we deal with our own human responses and the responses of others, may we have compassion, understanding and wisdom.

Affirmation: I am a human being. I am part of the human family on earth.

Prayer: O LORD, help our families to heal and be fully human. Give our military leaders and trainers wisdom and insight to use for our benefit and the benefit of humanity.

Reflections / Notes

MEDITATION 91

2 Kings 7:3-20

Unexpected Messengers – Telling the Truth

So they came and called to the gatekeepers of the city, and told them.
v.10

When there is a famine or drought in the land, people can become very desperate. Lack of food, be it physical, mental or spiritual can lead to malnutrition. Lack of water or 'bad water' can lead to long-term neurological-psychological damage, not just momentary disorientation and delusion.

Sometimes we don't know who to listen to, or what to believe is true. Sometimes the truth comes in unexpected packaging. Great life changing truths can come through those who we may see as 'outcasts', 'nobodies'- those who we thought were unimportant. Discerning and testing what we believe as truth is key. Listen and then check.

Affirmation: The mind of Christ and discernment of the Holy Spirit is with me.

Prayer: O LORD, thank You for Your mind and discernment in my life.

Reflections / Notes

MEDITATION 92

Chronicles 7:12-22

Healing the Nation

If my people who are called by my name humble themselves, pray, seek my face, and turn from their wicked ways, then will I hear from heaven and will forgive their sin and heal their land. v.14

When God's chastisement comes through the forces of creation, tragedy, or economic ruin, our moments become times for reflection. While we might be caught in the world-wind asking why is this happening to me and to you, we must humble ourselves and recognize that neither you nor I are the center of the universe.

In these times we need to kneel before an infinite God and pray. Seek the face of God – let God's Word show us where we have fallen short, and then turn from our wicked ways. Don't keep doing what we have been doing, but rather turn from that which is against the Scriptures.

If my people...then will God hear from heaven, forgive our sin and heal our land.

There are no short-cuts.

Affirmation: I will participate in my healing and the healing of my nation.

Prayer: O LORD, empower us through the working of your Holy Spirit to be faithful.

Reflections / Notes

MEDITATION 93

Isaiah 30: 18-26

God Heals

...on the day when the LORD binds up the injuries of the people, and heals the wounds inflicted by His blow. v.26

It will serve us well to once again read this complete Scriptural text. In it we learn that God is our Teacher. Though there may be adversity and affliction, God does not hide Himself from us. We will still be able to spiritually see our Teacher. We will still be able to spiritually hear the directions of our Teacher saying "This is the way; walk in it."

If there is idolatry of any kind in our midst, we are to get rid of it. When all is said and done, we are promised that we will experience clean water and flourishing crops to eat. We will have more than enough.

Affirmation: I will listen to what I believe God is saying to me, and do what I believe I should do.

Prayer: Thank you LORD for giving me direction, hope and fulfillment of purpose.

Reflections / Notes

MEDITATION 94

Psalm 111

Wisdom 101

The fear of the LORD is the beginning of wisdom; all those who practice it have a good understanding. His praise endures forever. v.10

Acknowledging and remembering that you are a human being and not Almighty God, is the key to strong mental health. Remembering that God Almighty has "got your back" – goes before you and is your rear guard, can reduce anxiety and fear.

Seeking and doing what God wants, no matter what the situation, brings the peace that passes all understanding. Resting in the fact that your mistakes and sins are forgiven through Jesus Christ gives strength to body, mind and spirit; and gives an unexplainable peace and joy. Knowing the Scriptures, and being enlightened and empowered through the working of the Holy Spirit of God in our lives, places each of us at an advantage in surmounting life's ups, and downs and all kinds of situations in between.

Affirmation: God grants me wisdom, strength, peace, joy and love each day.

Prayer: May me and my household acknowledge and remember to keep God first. May we walk guided by the Holy Scriptures and empowered by the Holy Spirit. May our intellects be enlightened by you O LORD. Thank You.

Reflections / Notes

Meditation 95

---

2 Corinthians 4: 5-12

Treasure in Clay Jars

But we have this treasure in clay jars (earthen vessels), so that it may be clear that its extraordinary power belongs to God and does not come from us. v.7

Human limitations remind us that we are made of clay —earth. Each of us must eat, sleep and heal when we are sick or our body is broken in some way. Each of us has emotions and feelings. No matter what our human condition, the Divine breath within us comes from God. And if there is any extraordinary power operating through us we know we are not the source. As children of the Light we link to the God of the Universe, not fallen angels, principalities and powers. We walk in the strength and power of the Divine.

That extra determination, tremendous idea; that warmth and love shared between human beings…the real source is the God of the Universe. As for those people working miracles in Jesus name, we know who the real source is, so let us not get caught up in worshipping a human being that God may be working through for his kingdom and glory.

Affirmation: The LORD is working mightily in and through me.

Prayer: Thank You for what you are doing in and through me, the lives of my family, people in our country and those around the world.

Reflections / Notes

John 4:46-54

No Matter What Your Economic Class

Now there was a royal official whose son lay ill in Capernaum... v.46b

Any adult or child can become ill. Physicians of the time may or may not be able to assist in the healing.

Like the official in the Scriptural text we were encouraged to go to the Great Physician – Jesus, the one sent from God. This man had traveled a great distance to ask Jesus to heal is son. This father was not distracted by the people who surrounded Jesus. He made the press.

In our day and time, we too are encouraged to go to Jesus. Seek him first, so he may order our footsteps in the healing process. With Jesus with us we can shoulder whatever the day may bring, because he shoulders it with us.

Affirmation: The LORD, is ordering my footsteps toward healing and recovery.

Prayer: Thank you LORD for being with us.

Reflections / Notes

Hebrews 11:27-28

Keep On Keeping On in God's Supernatural Strength

By faith he (Moses) left Egypt, unafraid of the king's anger; for he persevered as though he saw him who was invisible. v.27

Spending time alone in prayer – conversation with God can boost your perseverance. Prayer is a conversation.

You praise God for who God is and what God has done, and then you wait and listen to God from within you. The Holy Spirit makes this happen.

You say "thank you LORD", and then you listen. You ask God for something, and then you listen.

Discerning the voice of God can be essential for all of us. God is not going to tell you anything that contradicts the Scriptures. Reading, studying, knowing the Scriptures will help you discern the voice of God from all the other voices in your life – whether the voice is that of your, relative, friend, children, or your own negative or desirous thoughts.

A talk with God, can take you a long way.

Affirmation: I talk with God daily for at least 30 minutes.

Prayer: Thank You LORD for being there.

Reflections / Notes

MEDITATION 98

1 Kings 2:1-4, 10-12

Passing the Baton from Generation to Generation

I am about to go the way of all earth. Be strong, be courageous, and keep the charge of the LORD your God...so you will prosper in all that you do and wherever you turn. v2-3

David the father of Solomon is dying. During his last days on earth he gives his son Solomon his final instructions. It is a practice that our parents may have done with us and parents all over the world do with their children. In his last moments, he tries to say only that which is important...that which will sustain him as an individual, family or community. David is "passing the baton" to his son, so Solomon too can complete the journey of life well.

David's words echo for us even now in our time. "Be strong, be courageous, and keep the charge of the LORD your God." In other words, "be faithful to God"... "so you will prosper in all that you do, wherever you turn".

Again, be strong, be courageous and keep the charge of the LORD your God.

Affirmation: I will live my life, so my family knows how to live life faithful to the Living God.

Payer: O LORD, empower me to be wise, strong, courageous and faithful to you. Thank You.

Reflections / Notes

MEDITATION 99

Acts 22:1-16

The Power of Language

Speaking the language of a person or people is very strategic if you want to minister to them with the Gospel of Jesus the Christ or to provide any service to them. Communication is key in people getting to know one another.

Amazingly, throughout time people have used keywords with different groups of people to somewhat manipulate or get a certain response. Truly there is nothing new under the sun. Some people know just what "button to press" to get their desired response.

As children of God, let us listen to the real message. Does it line-up with the Scriptures – with God's agenda? Do the words and actions promote fullness of life, love and justice?

Affirmation: I will use wisdom, pray, and communicate in words and actions that promote God's love and justice. When I communicate with others I will connect.

Prayer: Help me LORD, to be faithful to you in all my communications in words and actions.

Reflections / Notes

Psalm 62

Pour Out Your Heart Before God – God is a Refuge for Us

Trust in Him at all times, O people; pour out your heart before him; God is a refuge for us. v8

Our God is a refuge, a safe place. God moves us into a safe place spiritually, mentally, and physically. God Almighty surrounds us spiritually and then working through others surrounds us with His people, with shelter and protection; and all our needs are met.

The power and steadfast love of the LORD continues to deliver you and me in many ways during the night and day.

Come into the place of rest and safety, the place of refuge.

Affirmation: God is my refuge and supplies a physical place of rest and safety.

Prayer: O LORD, thank you for being my refuge, my deliverer. I will trust you at all times. Thank You for Your strength.

Reflections / Notes

_____

_____

_____

_____

_____

_____

_____

_____

_____

_____

_____

_____

_____

_____

_____

_____

_____

_____

Prayer to Receive Jesus Christ as LORD and Savior and be Filled with the Holy Spirit

Prayer:

Almighty God, Creator, Redeemer and Sustainer, I thank you for sending Your Son Jesus the Christ to break the power of death and sin through the shedding of His blood, His death, and resurrection from the dead. Thank you for forgiving me all my sins. On this day I receive Jesus Christ as my LORD and Savior. I renounce the devil and all his ways and all his works.

Empower me by the working of your Holy Spirit to fulfill your purpose for me. Seal me and fill me with your Holy Spirit. In Jesus name I pray. Amen

Instructions:

Go to church to hear the Scriptures of God preached, be baptized, take communion (Lord's Supper), and gather with other Christians. Read and study the bible daily, praise and worship God daily. Love God with all your heart, mind and soul; and love your neighbor as yourself.

Prayer for Deliverance

In the name of Jesus, I bind-up every spirit of Satan and his co-workers and cast them into the pit of hell. Do not tare the human body when you exit. I loose in (name) life, obedience to the Living God as revealed in the Christian Scriptures. Fill (name) with Your Holy Spirit.
Thank You. In Jesus name I (we) pray. Amen.

Read: Ephesian 6:10-18

Lord's Prayer
(The prayer Jesus taught his disciples to pray)
Matthew 6:9-13

Our Father, who in heaven, hallowed be your name.

Your kingdom come, Your will be done on earth as it is in heaven.

Give us this day our daily bread.

And forgive us our debts (trespasses or sins), as we also have forgiven our debtors (those who trespass or sin against us).

And do not bring us to the time of trial (or into temptation), but rescue us from the evil one (evil).

For the kingdom, and the power and the glory are yours forever. Amen

About the Author

everend Michele Pearl Ellison, A.C.S.W., M.Div. served as a volunteer chaplain with children of US military personnel, whose parents were deployed in the Persian Gulf War. Her father served in the Pacific and later as Veterans of Foreign Wars Post founder and Commander. Her mother served as a dental hygienist at the VA Hospital, Northport, New York.

Ordained as a clergywoman in 1994, Rev. Ellison is a member of the Academy of Certified Social Workers (A.C.S.W.); and has worked as a mental health therapist/supervisor in New York and therapist in Washington, D.C. integrating Christian spirituality and mental health.

A Master of Social Work (M.S.W.) graduate of the State University of New York at Stony Brook, Rev. Ellison's social work career spans over 30 years. She received her Master of Divinity from Virginia Union University, School of Theology, Richmond, Va. and attended the Lutheran Theological Seminary at Gettysburg, Pa., with cross-studies at the Washington Theological Union, Washington D.C. and Presbyterian School of Christian Education. Rev. Ellison received her training in Clinical Pastoral Education at the Medical College of Virginia and Hospital Chaplaincy, Inc. a/k/a HealthCare Chaplaincy, Inc., New York, New York.

Trained as a multicultural writer by the Evangelical Lutheran Church in America, she has written devotionals that have been used nationally and internationally.

Rev. Ellison is a motivational/inspirational speaker and writer. She conducts workshops/seminars that enhance the healing and social functioning of individuals, families and communities.

A Benjamin E. Mays Fellow, she is listed in International Who's Who of Professionals (1997), and Who's Who Among Human Services Professionals (1988).

www.ingramcontent.com/pod-product-compliance
Lightning Source LLC
Chambersburg PA
CBHW021624120626
46545CB00002B/384